CAMBRIDG

MW01707097

CHEROKEE Leader

and Other Nonfiction Readings

Jack Warner

CAMBRIDGE Adult Education
A Division of Simon & Schuster
Upper Saddle River, New Jersey

Executive Editor: Mark Moscowitz
Editor: Robert McIlwaine
Production Director: Penny Gibson
Print Buyer: Cheryl Johnson
Production Editor: Alan Dalgleish
Book Design: Margarita T. Linnartz
Electronic Page Production: Maria Falkenberg
Electronic Art: Armando Baéz
Cover Design: Eric Dawson

Printed in the United States of America
1 2 3 4 5 6 7 8 9 10 99 98 97 96 95

ISBN 0-13-177452-2

CAMBRIDGE Adult Education
A Division of Simon & Schuster
Upper Saddle River, New Jersey

Contents

1

The Ashanti tribe of Africa's Gold Coast has a folklore admired the world over. A favorite figure in Ashanti tales is Kwaku Ananse [KWAH kyew un nun SEH], a rogue of a spider, whose fame as a folklore character has spread well beyond Africa.

How Wisdom Was Spread Throughout the World

Long, long ago—in fact, not long after the world itself was created—there was but one wise person. That was Kwaku Ananse, the spider. Sadly, though, Ananse was as greedy as he was wise, for he was determined to keep the wisdom of the world to himself.

After a long time spent guarding his wisdom, Ananse grew tired and bored. "I cannot go on like this," he lamented. "I am spending all my time guarding wisdom, not using it."

He thought and thought, and then came up with a plan. He would ask his wife, Aso (AH so), to make him a huge pot. He would stuff all of his wisdom into the pot and seal it. "Then I will be free to do as I please," Ananse said, "for I will no longer have to worry about anyone stealing my wisdom."

Aso dutifully went to the riverbank, where she dug clay. She shaped a huge pot, putting a very small opening at the top so her husband could seal it firmly. Then she rolled the pot out into the hot sun to bake. While the pot baked, she made a stopper for the tiny opening.

Once she was sure the pot had baked dry and hard, Aso carried it carefully back to her husband. Ananse looked it over very carefully, grunted his approval, and waved his wife away. When Aso had left, Ananse stuffed his wisdom deep into the pot, covered it with cocoa-yam leaves, and banged home the stopper. Then, to be sure no wisdom could escape, he tied the stopper down with strong vines.

Ananse stepped back to admire his work, when he quickly realized he should hide the pot somewhere. He settled on hiding it in the topmost branches of a tall silk-cotton tree, which he knew stood deep in the forest.

"The tree has spikes in its trunk. That will keep others from trying to climb it if they happen to see the pot hidden in the branches," Ananse said. With that, Ananse picked up the pot in his arms and set out into the forest. Because the pot was heavy, and he was being careful not to drop it, Ananse never noticed he was being followed by his small son, Ntikuma (tih KOO muh).

When Ananse reached the silk-cotton tree, he stopped to rest. The long hot walk carrying the pot heavy with wisdom had tired him. When he stopped, Ntikuma hid behind a nearby tree to see what would happen next.

Now fully rested, Ananse tied a vine to the pot, which he hung around the front of his neck. Then he stepped up to the tree.

Ananse stretched his arms out to get a grip on the tree in order to climb it. But because the pot was in the way, he could not reach the tree trunk. Grunting and sweating, Ananse tried this way and that to grasp the tree—to no avail. He tried and tried again, his grunting turning into howling and then into the loudest swearing as he grew hotter and more tired with each fruitless try.

Meanwhile, Ntikuma, watching from behind the nearby tree, could stand his father's howling and swearing no longer. He slipped up behind Ananse, unseen.

"Father," he said timidly, "if you wish to climb that tree, why not carry the pot on your back? Tied to your front as it is, there is no way your hands will be free to grasp the trunk."

Ananse's face grew darker with rage. His small son had taught him a lesson he knew was all too true. In fact, he was so angry, he grabbed at the pot. He meant to take it off, then punish his son for being disrespectful. But, alas, his hands were trembling with rage and wet with sweat. The heavy pot slipped out of his hands and crashed to the ground. It was shattered—all of its contents poured out.

At that very moment, a wind came up, blowing wisdom far and wide. The wind was soon followed by rain, which drove wisdom into the rivers that led to the sea. In this way wisdom was carried to the far corners of the world.

Kwaku Ananse set out after Ntikuma who, seeing the rage his father was in, fled toward home. Fresher now than his father, the small boy ran well ahead of his father. As Ananse staggered through the forest, he bellowed loudly at his son, blaming him for the misfortune. However, this was mostly bluffing, for in truth Ananse was not really angry at Ntikuma. "What good is owning all that wisdom," he admitted, "if my own small son can judge better than I?"

Focus on Reading

1. Ananse, the folktale says, was both wise and greedy. How does the folktale show that he was

wise? How does the folktale show that he was greedy?

2. Was Ananse's plan to hide the pot high in a silk-cotton tree a good one? Explain why, or why not.

3. Many folktales include a lesson for readers. What was the lesson Ananse learned from his adventure? How might the lesson Ananse learned apply to you?

2

Would you be willing to risk millions of dollars for the chance to win *billions*? If so, you would not be alone. Over the years hundreds of people have done just that in an amazing search for a buried treasure that may never have existed!

Oak Island's Mysterious Money Pit

Oak Island lies in Mahone, off the southern coast of Nova Scotia (No vah sko shah), itself a part of Canada. It is a small island, only one mile long and a half-mile wide. A peaceful home for birds, rabbits, and deer, Oak Island seems no different from the other 300 islands in the bay. But it is indeed different. Oak Island is the center of one of the greatest treasure hunts the world has ever known.

It all began some 200 years ago. On a warm summer's day in 1795, 16-year-old Daniel McGinnis set out to explore Oak Island, then uninhabited by people. When he found part of a ship's ropes and pulleys hanging from the limb of an oak tree, the boy became quite excited. Under the ship's gear was a bowl-shaped dent in the earth, perhaps 12 feet across. "Buried treasure, pirate's treasure!" Dan shouted.

The next day he returned to the island with two friends, and the digging began. Soon their shovels uncovered what looked like a mine shaft of some kind. Ten feet into the shaft, they hit upon a platform of rotted logs. They continued to dig—harder and faster now, spurred on by their early finds. They dug and dug—all summer and well into the fall months. Then the weather got too cold, so they quit.

When Dan and his friends returned the next spring, they knew they would need help. But no one would join them. "Fools," they were called. The boys shrugged off the names and, whenever they could find the time, worked for eight long, hard years at their digging.

Then, in 1803, they got help. A man named Simeon Lynds joined in the dig. He brought machinery, other men, and money as well. Simeon Lynds' diggers continued to find log platforms every few feet. They also found one covered with charcoal, a second with putty, and another with some kind of threads of fiber. But no treasure.

Then, when the pit was 90 feet deep, they came across the first of several clues that something important was in the pit. This was a flat stone, about 3 feet long and 1 foot wide. A series of strange marks were cut into the stone. Could this be some kind of code?

It could indeed, some experts stated. One translated the markings into a message: "Forty feet below two million pounds are buried." (In today's money that means hundreds of millions of dollars—at least!) Dan, his friends, and Simeon were convinced they could soon be rich. However, at the 98-foot level, disaster struck. Overnight, the shaft Simeon and his men dug filled with water. No amount of pumping could stop the flow. Simeon Lynds gave up the dig.

For the next 45 years, Oak Island's money pit lay untouched. Then, in 1849, a second group was formed to search for the treasure—if indeed there was one to find.

This group was led by a man named Jotham McCully. In 12 days McCully's crew dug another shaft to a depth of 84 feet. At that point, water flooded the shaft and the men were nearly drowned.

Where was the water coming from? McCully found the answer in a nearby beach. Under the stones that covered the beaches were layers of eel grass and some kind of other material. Then he found five rock-walled drains leading toward the pit. The drains formed a flood trap designed to keep the money pit filled with sea water!

It took a genius to think up such a plan. It certainly must have taken a good deal of hard work to carry it out. Experts later said it would have taken 100 diggers at least six months to build the system.

That made McCully even more sure that something important was buried in the pit. What could it be? Who could have done the burying?

Over the years any number of people have made their guesses. Some people think Queen Elizabeth I of England was behind the plan. These people think she wanted to hide treasure she took from Spain 400 years ago. Others think pirates may have buried treasure in the pit. Both William Kidd, the pirate known as "Captain Kidd," and the evil pirate Blackbeard had great treasures. Both died before anyone learned where they hid their treasures—if they did.

Another idea is that Oak Island may have been a bank for a number of pirates. Pirates have been known to band together to hide their treasure. The money pit looks something like other pirate banks in other parts of the world. Finally, some people say the whole thing is a big practical joke. There is no treasure, and there never was.

McCully was not one of the last group, though. So he thought up a new plan. This time he would drill a hole to the flood tunnel. Then he would seal it off. That way no more water could get into the main pit.

The plan might have worked, except for one thing. McCully did not know there were many flood tunnels. Twice he dug and twice his men fled for their lives as water rushed into the pit. That was enough for Jotham McCully. He quit.

No sooner had McCully left than others took his place. Some interesting finds occurred. In 1897 pieces of paper were found 155 feet down. They were two letters, written with an old pen on an old kind of paper called parchment. But what did they mean?

Later, another crew struck iron plating. Could this be a chest with gold and jewels? Still later, pieces of old wire and metal were brought up. But no treasure.

Group after group tried and quit. Among those the pit defeated were a millionaire, a teacher, a drilling engineer—and the Restall family from England. Sadly, Mr. Restall, his son, and two of their workers were killed in the pit. And still no treasure.

If there is a treasure buried on Oak Island, a man named David Tobias is determined he will find it. Tobias heads a group that is still digging on the island—more than 200 holes so far. The only items his workers have brought up are iron spikes and some old pairs of scissors.

But Tobias is not discouraged. He is willing to spend $10 million on his latest plan. This will be a huge shaft, 80 feet wide and 200 feet deep. It will be big enough to include all the older shaftsdug back to the time of Dan McGinnis and Simeon Lynds. What about the problem of water flooding into his shaft? Tobias believes huge pumps will keep up with the flow.

Will Tobias succeed where others have failed? Only time will tell. Time and, perhaps, a legend that has grown up around Oak Island's mysterious money pit. That legend says any treasure will be found only after all the red oak trees on the island have died, or only after seven lives have been lost in the pit. Today, a few red oaks remain, standing near the more than 30 shafts that have been dug. In the pit itself, the bodies of Robert Restall, his son, and two workers still lie.

Focus on Reading

1. What were the main risks for men digging for buried treasure in Oak Island's money pit?
2. Have you ever gotten involved in a get-rich-quick plan? What happened? What do you think of it now? Do you know people who have succeeded in one of them?
3. Is there a moral lesson to be learned from this article on the search for buried treasure? What would you say it was?

3

Inventors, someone once said, have "wondering minds." One such inventor, an African American man named Garrett A. Morgan, used his wondering mind to invent a number of useful products. Two of those have saved untold numbers of lives over the years.

GET GARRETT MORGAN!

Like most large cities, Cleveland, Ohio, has a network of tunnels deep under its streets. But unlike many other cities, some of Cleveland's tunnels run under water as well. One of these is the Cleveland Waterworks Tunnel 5. Tunnel 5 lies some 250 feet under the surface of Lake Erie, along whose shores the city of Cleveland sits.

On the morning of July 25, 1916, a work crew of more than 30 men descended into number 5. They were sent to inspect the tunnel and to do some routine maintenance.

For much of the day the men worked steadily, cleaning, digging, patching, looking for weak spots in the tunnel's walls. As they worked, the men were completely unaware that deadly gases were building up around them. Then, just before the first shift of workers was about to be replaced, a violent explosion thundered through the tunnel.

What caused the gases to explode, no one knows. It could have been a spark from a worker's pick or shovel. It could have been a short circuit in the tunnel's lighting system. Perhaps it was even caused by someone lighting a match.

Whatever the cause, the results were disastrous. Parts of the tunnel's walls collapsed, dropping huge clouds of dust and debris on the now-trapped workers. To make matters even worse, the deadly gases began to build up once again. What pure air was left in the tunnel would soon be poisoned—if more explosions didn't happen sooner. If something wasn't done soon, everyone trapped in the tunnel would surely die.

The explosion had been hearded all over Cleveland. Within minutes, a growing crowd of people reached the entrance of Tunnel 5. A few of the braver ones even tried to enter the tunnel itself. No sooner had they passed out of the sight of the onlookers than they reappeared. This time they were gasping for breath and coughing heavily. There was no way anyone could breathe in that burning hell of fire and smoke.

A collective moan rose from the crowd once they realized how serious things were. Grown men turned away, eyes reddened with tears. Their friends and relatives were trapped in number 5, and there was nothing anyone could do to help them.

Then someone—to this day, no one knows who it was—remembered seeing a demonstration of a gas mask a few months before. The inventor had shown his mask as a way to build interest in it. It had even won a prize at a fair in New York City. Still, no one seemed interested in the invention. But on that terrible July day in Cleveland, Ohio, Garrett Morgan's gas mask would prove to be a lifesaver.

"Get Garrett Morgan!" the man cried out. "He can help!" Someone else in the crowd who knew Garrett Morgan sprinted to his house. Gasping for breath after the long run, he hastily explained the situation in the tunnel. He ended by saying, "Someone said you have a gas mask. Whatever that is, bring it!"

Garrett nodded, then called to his brother Frank, who was in another room. Together they gathered four masks and hurried to the tunnel entrance.

Garrett and Frank slipped on two of the masks and started for the tunnel. As they did, two other men stepped forward. "Show us how to use the mask, so we can help," they pleaded.

Garrett gave the two men a quick lesson, then all four clambered down into the tunnel. In minutes they were back, each carrying an unconscious worker. Again and again they went back into the tunnel carrying out the victims. Before the day was over, they brought out 32 men, all of whom recovered.

For his heroics, Garrett Morgan was given a gold medal \ with diamonds by the city of Cleveland. What is more, word of the rescues using the gas mask spread across the country. Soon orders for the Morgan Mask flowed in from fire departments.

A number of places asked for Morgan himself to speak and to demonstrate his invention. He did so, willingly. But when people saw he was African American, they canceled their orders. No matter how good the gas mask was, many cities and towns refused to buy it-only because the inventor was African American.

Many other people would have been angered, or would have given up the invention completely. But not Garrett Morgan: he knew he had invented a device that would save lives. So he kept on selling it, even if he had to use white men in the demonstrations.

Today, firefighters everywhere use this equipment that allows them to breathe in dangerous environments. So do soldiers, whose equipment protects them from deadly war gases. In fact, so do any workers whose jobs put them in places where pure air is not available use them. All these people have Garrett Morgan to thank.

If the gas mask had been Garrett Morgan's only invention, it would have insured him a place in history. However, he had many more ideas he turned into useful products. Those range in importance from one of the first successful hair colorings (for people who hated to see their hair turn gray) to an automated traffic light.

The idea for the traffic light came to Garrett Morgan this way. Garrett was driving his car in Cleveland when he saw an accident. A car and a horse-drawn wagon crashed into each other at a busy intersection. He looked at the signal setup at the crossroads and knew right away what caused the crash.

The traffic signal, like all the others of the time, had only two positions. These were *stop* and *go*. There was no yellow caution light as traffic signals have today. What is more, the traffic signal could not be seen clearly from all four roads that met at the intersection. Finally, a traffic officer, who was suppose to regulate the changes, was not at his post. In fact, he was absent more often than he was on duty. As a result, people simply ignored the signal.

That evening, Garrett sketched out some rough ideas at home. Then he built a full-sized model. His work was good enough to earn him a *patent*, written proof from the government giving him the sole right to make and sell his invention, in 1923. After that, Cleveland put up his traffic lights. Soon other cities followed, and the name of Garrett Morgan was at the top again.

Just who was this Garrett Morgan? He was born in Paris, Kentucky, on March 4, 1877. His mother had been an African American slave, set free by President Abraham Lincoln's Emancipation Proclamation in 1863.

Garrett went to school through the sixth grade. Then he had to quit to help his brothers and sisters run the family farm. When he was 14 years old, Garrett left home for Cincinnati, Ohio, where he worked at a number of different jobs—and where he hired someone to help him learn to read and speak better. In 1895, he was on to Cleveland, the city where he spent the rest of his life.

If Garrett Morgan had one other outstanding quality besides a wondering mind, it was his love of tinkering. Perhaps in his case, at least, the two went hand in hand. Give him a machine of any kind—sewing machine, electric motor, what have you—and

Garrett would be certain to pull it apart. He always loved to know how something worked, and he always wondered if he could make it work better.

That describes Garrett Morgan the inventor. What about Garrett Morgan the man? Perhaps no one summed up the kind of person Garrett was better than his granddaughter Karen did a few months after his death in 1963.

Her grandfather, Karen wrote, "was a down-to-earth practical man. He worked hard for everything he ever did or accomplished. With all his achievements, one fact remained to be true until his last breath. He was proud to be an American, proud of his race."

Focus on Reading

1. Garrett Morgan was not only smart, but he was a brave man. Explain how the story shows Garrett's courage.
2. When some fire departments learned it was an African American man who invented the gas mask, they canceled their orders. How did Garrett Morgan react? How would you have reacted?
3. Suppose you met Garrett Morgan. What one thing would you tell him he should invent? Why?

4

Every day of our lives we benefit from many seemingly simple things, which, in fact, require great effort on the part of many people to bring into existence. Here is the story of one such common product, first introduced in the United States in 1847.

STAMPS FOR AMERICANS

What do Elvis Presley, rocks, and W.E.B. DuBois have in common? Most people would likely say, "Not much." But if you are one of the country's 19 million philatelists, or stamp collectors, you know the answer. Each of these has been the subject of a postage stamp.

If Elvis Presley is honored by a postage stamp, why not, say, Janis Joplin, or Gloria Estefan? How on earth did something like petrified wood deserve such an honor? The answer lies in a group of people known as the CSAC—the Citizens Stamp Advisory Committee.

For more than 35 years (since 1957), the CSAC has chosen which subjects will appear on postage stamps in the United States, and which will not appear. Every two months, this 14-member committee meets in Washington, D.C. to examine and discuss ideas for postage stamps.

The committee includes artists, historians, celebrities, ordinary people and, yes, stamp collectors. The committee reviews the choices and picks the ones it feels should become stamps. Then it sends its choices along to the Postmaster General, who has the final say. (In practice, though, the Postmaster General usually accepts the designs the CSAC picks.) Whatever decision—yes or no—is made on a particular idea, there is no appeal. Nor is any reason for accepting or turning down an idea given.

Still, there are guidelines the CSAC follows in choosing subjects for stamps. The guidelines, set up by the Postal Service, include the following:

• No living persons will be honored.

• Former presidents become eligible one year after their death. (Everyone else must wait at least ten years.)

• Only ideas that have widespread national appeal and importance will be chosen.

• No businesses, specific products, religious groups, or charities will be chosen.

• No anniversaries of towns, cities, schools, or colleges will be selected.

Anyone may submit an idea for a stamp, and lots of people do. In fact, the Postal Service gets about 3,000 letters a year from people who have ideas for stamps. The range of ideas is great. One from a student in Colorado thought "it would be nice to have a stamp showing a man on horseback going through town yelling, 'Colorado is 100 years old!'" Another was from a youngster in Seattle, Washington, who demanded "a ten-cent teddy bear stamp" because "the teddy bear has been the symbol of children's toys for hundreds of years." He ended his letter by saying, "The kids of this country want a teddy bear stamp!" Neither idea was accepted, by the way.

Of course, not all ideas for stamps come from individuals. A great many are sent in by special interest groups. Some of these groups use new ways to try to sway the CSAC to their way of thinking. For example, onion growers wanted very much to have a stamp honoring that sharp-tasting vegetable. Along with their letter, the growers sent a sack of onions to each committee member. Despite their efforts, the onion stamp idea was rejected, too.

While the onion growers were no doubt saddened, theirs was not the only idea turned down. (As a matter of fact, only some 40 or so ideas end up becoming stamps each year.) Other ideas rejected recently include one for a stamp honoring the game of horseshoes; one noting the invention of barbed wire, the wire with sharp points used for fences on many American farms; and one marking the building of Palm Springs, California's, 10,000th swimming pool.

Having been turned down once is no reason to stop trying, however. A notable example is the woman who wrote the committee year after year arguing for a series of stamps showing rocks. (Her husband, it seems, was a geologist, a scientist who studies—you guessed it—rocks.) Her persistence finally paid off when the Postal Service did in fact issue a set of ten-cent stamps illustrated with various rocks.

So, what kind of ideas for stamps are most likely to be accepted? The CSAC likes to see ideas that will result in large, colorful stamps. It especially likes to see ideas that won't offend anyone (It is admittedly hard to please everybody. "You can find something to pick apart in any idea," one committee member recently explained.) One example of a design that everyone liked was the sheet picturing state birds and flowers. That was a particular favorite of collectors and users alike.

Well then, if birds and flowers are such popular subjects, it should follow that animals will be too. Right? Well, yes and no. In 1989, the Postal Service issued a Prehistoric Animals series with great publicity at Disney World. Shortly after that event, trouble came. Some experts claimed one of the dinosaurs on the stamps was misnamed. Others said not so. The argument carried on for months, and never was really settled. The sale of the stamps, which was very slow at first, picked up when people took notice of the stamps. They were big and colorful. Soon people forgot the arguments of the experts and bought the stamps. The

Prehistoric Animals series ended up another bestseller for the Postal Service—thanks to the publicity surrounding the misnamed dinosaur.

Bestselling issues is something the Postal Service is eager to have these days. In a time when the Service is losing money each year, any savings they can come up with translates into money in the bank. So, the more stamps they sell without having them stuck on letters and packages, the closer the Postal Service comes to making a profit.

For example, it costs more than 25 cents to deliver a first class letter. But if a million people buy sheets of 29-cent stamps to stick in an album or give as gifts, the Postal Service will realize millions of dollars in income without having to provide any real service!

Given that, it is no surprise the push is on for stamp ideas that will appeal both to collectors and to the general public. (This may help explain why fans of Elvis Presley finally won their fight for a stamp.) It also means the service is determined to turn out prettier, even better designed stamps. (One small step in this direction, you may have noticed, is dropping the cent sign after the numerals giving the value of the stamp. Eliminating the '¢' results in a sleeker design, the explanation goes.)

Producing prettier, better designed stamps means persuading the very best artists to carry ideas through to the final design. Since being chosen to design a stamp is considered a great honor, the Postal Service has been able to sign up a number of top artists.

As with the original idea, the artist's design is first approved by the Postmaster General and the CSAC. Then the design is sent to the Bureau of Printing and Engraving in Washington, D.C. (where, incidentally, paper money is also printed). Modern presses at the Bureau turn out as many as 200,000 stamps an hour using as many as nine different colors.

Once the sheets of stamps are printed, they are sent through a perforating machine. This machine punches tiny holes in the paper between the stamps so they can be separated easily. Then it's off to another machine, this one to put glue on the back of the stamps. Finally, the stamps are cut into smaller sheets (or bound into booklets), packaged, and sent to the local post offices.

Every step in the process of making stamps is checked, double-checked, then checked again. Sharp-eyed inspectors pore over every stamp looking for errors. If they find any, the stamps are immediately shredded. Yet every now and then errors get by the inspectors. After all, they are human, and humans do make mistakes.

It is errors that stamp collectors really hope to find on stamps. Errors, you see, greatly increase the value of a stamp. The most famous error in U.S. postage stamp history happened in 1918. That was the year a 24-cent airmail stamp carried a picture of an airplane. Unfortunately for the Postal Service (but fortunate indeed for collectors) a number of these stamps were printed with the airplane upside down. Before long this 24-cent stamp rose in value to $35,000! Today the inverted airmail stamp is worth even more.

Obvious errors like that are not the only way postage stamps increase their value either. Collectors have come up with a term—EFOs, or "Errors, Freaks, and Oddities"—to describe even minor mistakes. These include misplaced perforations that cut through a stamp, stamps that haven't been perforated, color variations between the same stamps, even cracks in a printing plate that result in tiny imperfections on the finished stamp. All these, and more, are important to collectors.

Then there are the rare stamps. These are the stamps most in demand by serious—and rich—collectors. Perhaps the most famous of rare stamps is the so-called British one-cent magenta, named for its original face value and color. First issued in 1856, this tiny (and ugly) little stamp sold several years ago for $280,000. Today it is worth much more than that. Crazy? Not to a serious collector. You see, there is only one known one-cent magenta in existence. Now that's a rare stamp!

So, the next time you go to stick a stamp on a letter, take a really close look at it. Even if you don't find any EFOs, you'll be looking at a miniature work of art. That fact alone deserves our attention.

Focus on Reading

1. What one bit of information from the article surprised you the most? Tell why.
2. "You can find something to pick apart in any idea," a CSAC member once said. What do you think the statement means? Do you agree with the comment? Why, or why not? Can you think of examples from your life when people have picked apart an idea?
3. If you were asked to submit an idea for a new stamp, what would your choice of subject be? Would it be a person? A place? An important event? Something else? Explain your choice.

5

One of the most amazing hoaxes of all time was carried off over 200 years ago in New York City by a man known only by the name Lozier, and his friend, "Uncle John" DeVoe.

Sawing Off Manhattan Island

The wrinkled old man leaned toward his friend sitting on the park bench. He looked this way and that, as if someone might try to hear what he was about to say. Then he spoke in a whisper.

"'Uncle John,' I have an idea."

John DeVoe put down his newspaper and looked back at the old man, whose eyes crinkled as he smiled. "Lozier," he said, "whenever I see that look in your eyes, I know someone is going to pay for it. I only hope it will not be me."

Lozier ignored his friend's comment. He stuck his face close to DeVoe's ear and began explaining his idea. As he listened, DeVoe's questioning eyes took on an amused look. Before the old man finished, DeVoe was trying his best to stop laughing.

"Shhh!" Lozier cautioned his friend. "Do you want everyone to know what we're up to?"

"We?" DeVoe questioned.

"Of course you, Uncle John. I'll need your help on this one."

"But what shall I do?" DeVoe asked.

"Just follow my lead" was the answer Lozier gave him.

With that, Lozier stood up and made an announcement addressed as much to the other men sitting on the benches as it was to Uncle John DeVoe. "Come, Uncle John," he said, "are you forgetting we have an important meeting to attend?"

Still not quite sure what was happening, DeVoe rose from the bench and followed his friend.

All this took place in the summer of 1824 at a place called Centre Market in Manhattan, a section of New York City. In those simpler days, New York City was much smaller than it is today. The people then were simpler, too, far more likely to believe than to question.

Centre Market itself was a favorite place of retired New Yorkers, who passed the hours telling stories to each other, and no one's stories were listened to more seriously than those the man named Lozier told.

He was, everyone believed, wiser, richer, and better educated than they were. After all, Lozier had been around the world many times as a ship's carpenter. Now he wore fine clothes, spoke several languages, drank fine wines, and ate at the city's top restaurants. What is more, he knew all the right people.

When Lozier and Uncle John DeVoe left Centre Market that July day, they did not return for nearly a week. When they returned, they acted strangely. They sat apart from the others, talking only between themselves, speaking quietly. All the while, they wore very serious looks.

After a day or two of this had passed, one of the regulars got up enough courage to ask why the two men were acting so oddly. At first, neither would offer an explanation. Finally, Lozier spoke.

"It is because we have had a number of meetings with Stephen Allen, the mayor of this great city."

"About what?" the man asked.

Lozier and DeVoe looked at each other, then nodded. "About the fact that Manhattan is too heavy on the south end, the Battery," DeVoe offered.

"So much so," Lozier broke in, "that there are signs it might break off and sink into the ocean. If that happens, there will be no counting the loss of life and property!"

By now a fair-sized group had gathered around the bench Lozier and DeVoe occupied. A voice piped up. "Hah! Likely story, that."

Lozier looked at the speaker. "You do not believe us?" he asked. "Why then, good sir, is the walk from City Hall to the Battery all downhill?"

That point, along with Lozier's reputation as a wise man, was enough to silence the questioner. A murmur of alarm went through the group. "What can be done to prevent this?" an anxious voice cried out.

Lozier raised a hand to calm everyone. "That is what Uncle John and I were talking to the mayor about," he said. "And we have a plan. We will simply saw Manhattan off at Kingsbridge, on the northern end. Then we will swing the island around so that the Battery is in the north and Kingsbridge in the south. Then we will anchor the Battery to the mainland."

"And that will keep it from sinking—forever," DeVoe added.

A collective gasp rose from the crowd. "Won't this be a gigantic job, perhaps impossible?" they asked. "How will the city do this?"

"Impossible?" Lozier asked. "Why not so long ago, people said the Erie Canal would never be built. The mountains stood in the way. But, as we speak, that canal is very nearly complete."

"And how many people laughed when it was said that steamships would someday cross the oceans? But they are, this very day!" DeVoe said.

The crowd was getting excited now, so Lozier held his hand up once more for silence. "We are the ones who will accomplish this," he said. "Mayor Allen insists that this be a private matter, with no government interference."

The crowd was hooked completely. They wanted to know what they could do to help save Manhattan. Lozier told them. He and DeVoe would organize the whole thing. First, they would need workers, hundreds of them, and food, tools, and special gear. After saying all that, Lozier and DeVoe left the market. They returned the next day.

Lozier carried a large book, which he handed to DeVoe. Uncle John would write down the name of every man who wanted to work on the project. Soon he had more than 300 names, all eager to get back to work in a time when work was scarce.

Meanwhile, Lozier made the rounds of butcher shops asking to buy food. He would need, he figured, 500 head of cattle, 500 hogs, and at least 3,000 chickens.

"Especially the chickens," Lozier told the butchers. "You see, I have promised the workers two chicken dinners a day, and I am a man of my word!"

Then he was off to the lumberyards. He would need enough lumber to erect a building to house hundreds of workers. He would need even more lumber for a second building, this one for the 20 or 30 cooks and laundry help he would hire.

No one questioned Lozier's orders, nor even doubted they would be paid. In fact, some owners were so eager to please him that they hauled loads of lumber to Kingsbridge on their own, where it was stacked and made ready for the project.

Next came the matter of tools, starting with the great saws. These would have to be specially made. Each was to be 100 feet long, with teeth 3 feet high. He would need 20 of these saws, and 50 men to work each one.

There were also the oars to row Manhattan once it was sawed free. There would be 24 oars, each one 250 feet long. Twelve would be set into huge oarlocks on the Hudson River side of Manhattan. The other 12 would be put on the East River side of the island. One hundred men would row Manhattan down the bay, turn it around, and row it back into place. An arrangement of chains and anchors would be set up to keep the island from floating out to sea in the event of a bad storm.

Lozier took his plans for these tools to a number of blacksmiths. men who made horseshoes. All of them immediately began figuring out how to build the tools and other metal equipment, and how much they would cost to make. Finally, Lozier sent out word that he was ready to hire the rowers and the men who would actually saw Manhattan free. They were to meet him and DeVoe in Centre Market for their final tests.

Lozier announced, "There will be extra pay for any man strong enough to be able to work under water!"

Within hours of the news reaching the streets of New York, Centre Market was swarming with eager hopefuls. Every day for a week, Lozier sat on his favorite bench. He timed man after man as they stepped forward and held their breath. Beside him, Uncle John DeVoe carefully entered the times in his book. Those who held their breath the longest were added to a special list. These were the names of workers who would get extra pay.

At last, everything was ready. Lozier gave out contracts for the buildings, the tools, the special gear, the food, and all the rest. He told everyone involved in the project where and when to meet.

"Tomorrow morning, at the corner of Bowery and Spring Streets, there will be a fife-and-drum band to play music and lead you all to Kingsbridge, where the work will begin!"

No one knows how many people actually showed up the next day. The best guesses place the number at between 500 and 1,000 men, many with their wives and children. Then there were the builders riding wagons loaded with lumber and tools, and butchers herding cattle and hogs. There were carts piled high with crates of live chickens. In short, nearly anyone who heard about the plan was there. Everyone, that is, except Lozier and Uncle John DeVoe. Those two left word they could not make the march because of ill health.

Without anyone to start things going, all those people and carts and wagons and animals began milling about the Bowery and Spring Streets. This went on for a few hours—until a few people finally caught on. Lozier and DeVoe had played a monstrous hoax.

As word spread through the crowds, most people simply gave up and headed off for home. A few, though, vowed to find the two crooks. "If we can't saw off Manhattan Island, at least we can saw off Lozier and DeVoe!" was their cry of outrage.

Search they did, but the hotheads never did find Lozier and DeVoe. In truth, they were hiding in a friend's house in Brooklyn, another section of New York City.

It was months before Lozier and DeVoe came out of hiding. By then, no one who had been fooled was willing to admit to the fact. So the two men never were punished for their hoax. However, when they finally got up enough nerve to return to Centre Market, no one would listen to anything they had to say.

Focus on Reading

1. A good title hints at what a selection is about, and, at the same time, it makes us want to read. Does "Sawing Off Manhattan Island" fit that description of a title? What might serve as another title for this true story?

2. What reasons can you think of for anyone to create a hoax? Give your own definition of a hoax. Can you give examples from your own experience?

3. Put yourself in the place of one of the people taken in by Lozier's hoax. How would you have felt? What would you have done? Ask yourself the same questions about another hoax (or other hoaxes) you know about from reading or your own experience.

6

Remedies for people with faulty eyesight go back in time many centuries. They ranged from looking at objects through quartz **crystals** to hanging a cow's eye around the neck. Today, expertly designed eyeglasses correct most defects quite nicely. But how do they work?

How Eyeglasses Help You See

If you're like one in three Americans (that's about 98 million people), you wear some kind of eyeglasses to help you see better. Why is it so many people have trouble seeing things clearly? To understand that, you have to know something about how the eyes work. Put simply, the eyes work very much like a camera. (See Figure 1.)

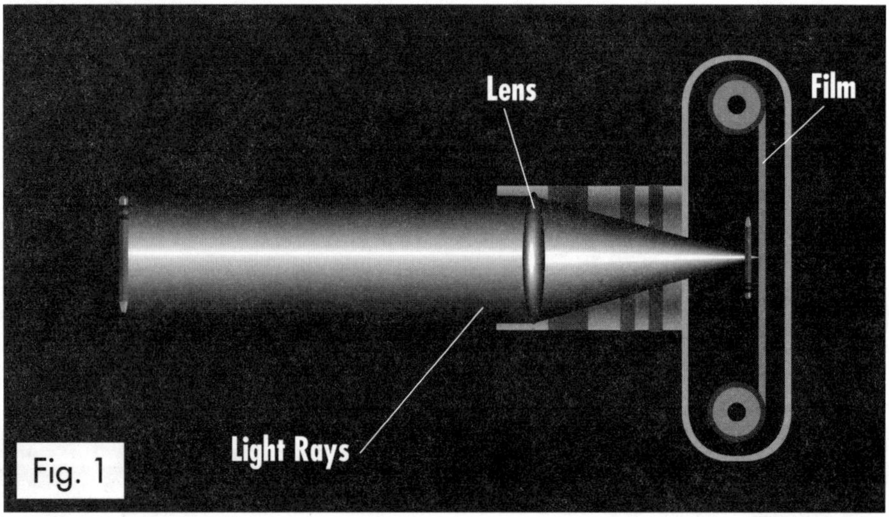

Fig. 1

A camera takes a picture on the film that has been loaded into it. Rays of light pass through the curved lens of the camera. As the light rays pass through the **lens**, they are bent. To get a clear image of the object being photographed, the person taking the picture **focuses**, or adjusts, the lens by moving it backward or forward until the object is perfectly clear. When that happens, he or she clicks a shutter and the light rays form an upside-down picture of the object on the film.

The human eye is really a natural camera. (See Figure 2.) It has a *cornea*, a kind of curved "window" that helps protect the eye. It has an *iris*, the colored part of the eye. In the center of the iris is the *pupil*. The pupil lets light into the *lens*. When the light is bright, the pupil remains quite small. But when the light is dim, the pupil widens to let in more light. These light rays pass through the pupil to the *lens* which, like the cornea, is curved. At the back of the eye is the *retina*. The retina acts like the film in a camera. It is where the image of the object being looked at appears. And like a camera, the image on the retina is upside-down. But as soon as the image appears on the retina, a signal is sent to the brain. The brain then turns the image rightside-up and enlarges it to full size. All this happens in less than an instant.

The lens of a camera, you will remember, is focused by the person taking the picture. The lens in a human eye, however, focuses itself by changing its shape. When you look at something far away, the lens gets thinner. When you look at something up close, the lens gets thicker. That way, people with good eyesight always see objects clearly. So why do some people have trouble seeing things clearly?

Usually the problem lies in the shape of the eyeball itself. For example, many people have trouble seeing objects that are far away. These people are *nearsighted*. That means they can see objects up close quite clearly, but far away objects appear fuzzy.

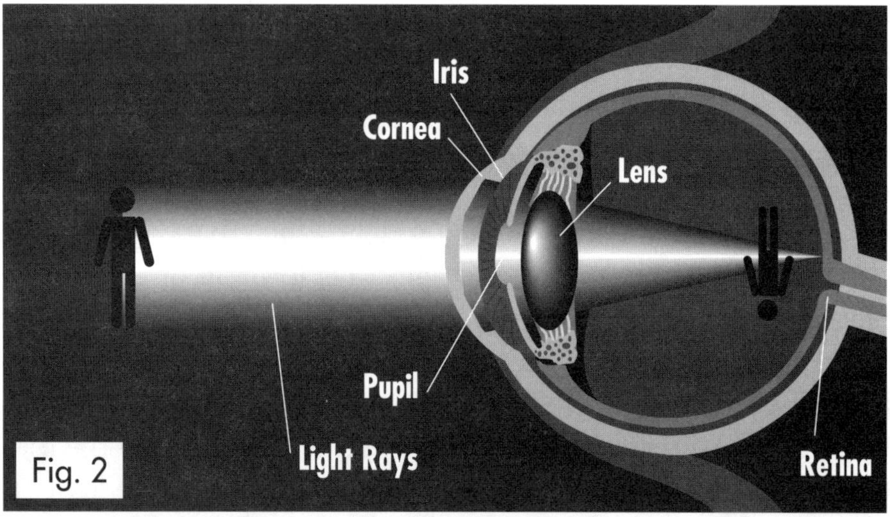

Fig. 2

The reason is their eyeballs are too long. Because of this, the lens cannot focus properly, and the image falls short of the retina. (See Figure 3.)

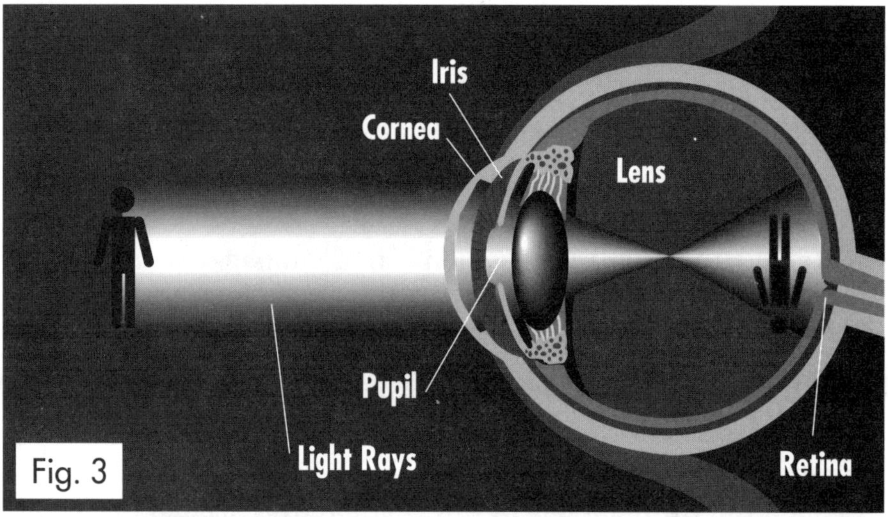

Fig. 3

To correct this, nearsighted people wear eyeglasses with *concave lenses*. Concave lenses are thinner in the middle than at the edges. As a result, the light rays passing through the lens bend less sharply. The image then falls directly on the retina. (See Figure 4.)

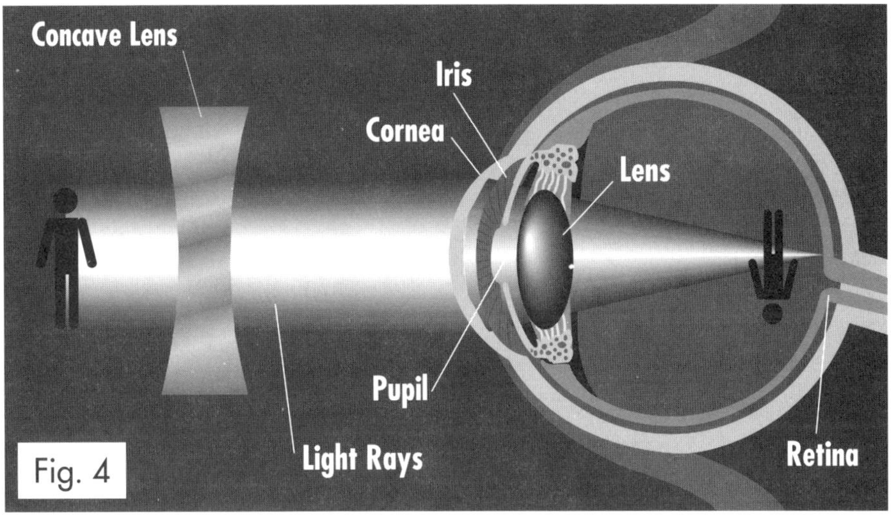

Fig. 4

People who can see faraway objects clearly while objects close to them are fuzzy are *farsighted*. In farsighted people, the eyeball is to short. Now the image falls beyond the retina. (See Figure 5.)

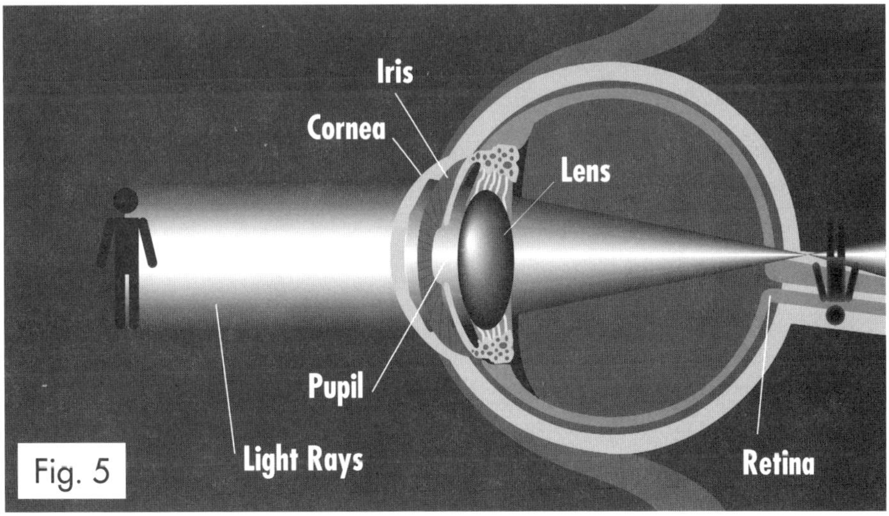

Fig. 5

To correct for farsightedness, people wear eyeglasses with convex lenses. Because convex lenses are thicker in the middle than at the edges, they bend the light rays quite sharply. As a result, a clear image of the object falls directly on the retina. (See Figure 6.)

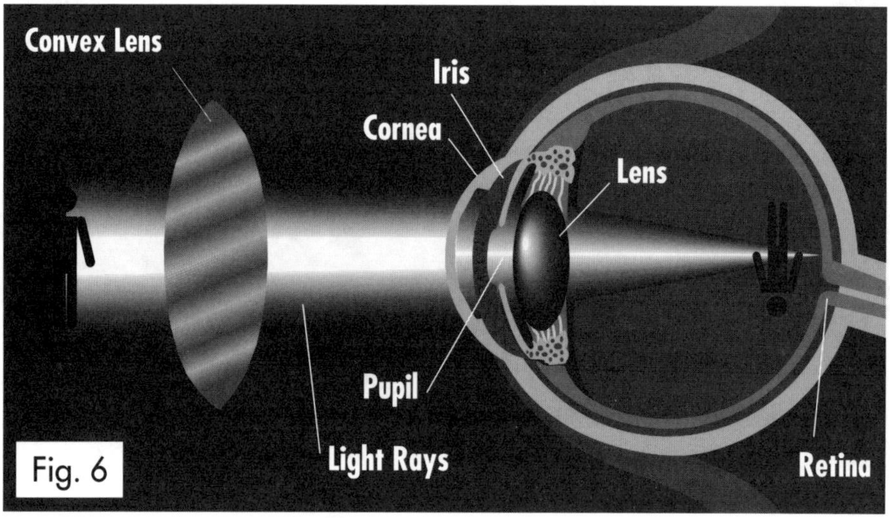

Fig. 6

A third, and also common, defect in eyes is *astigmatism*. Astigmatism is the result of the cornea or the lens not being perfectly round. When this occurs, the image on the retina will be blurred. Once again, eyeglasses will correct an astigmatism. A lens shaped like **cylinder** will do the job. (See Figure 7.)

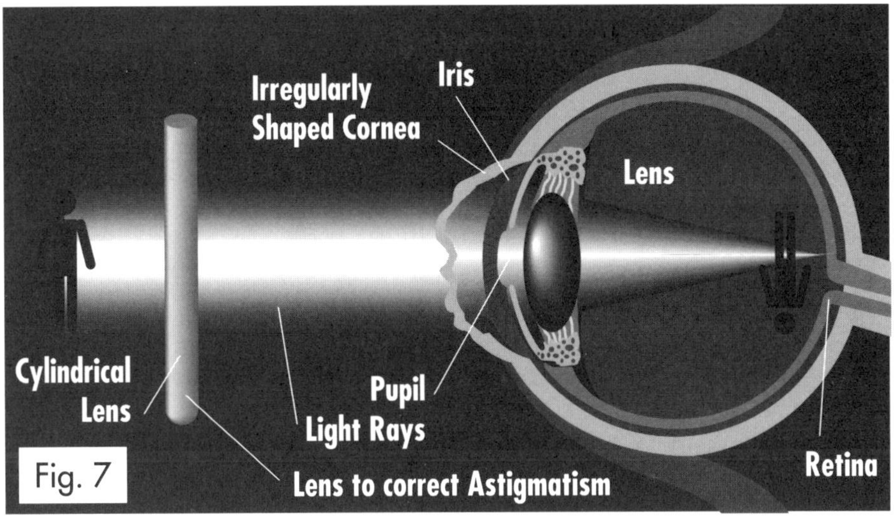

Fig. 7

A very simple test has been devised to tell if one or both of your eyes are astigmatic. The test is reproduced in Figure 8, the wheel diagram. Simply cover one eye and look at the diagram. If some of the **spokes** are gray and some black, the eye is astigmatic. Now do the same for the other eye.

Fig. 8

Fortunately nearsightedness, farsightedness, and astigmatisms are easily corrected with the proper eyeglass lenses. And people today accept eyeglasses as an everyday part of living. Indeed, a huge industry has grown up around "designer fashions" in eyewear, and sunglasses, whether to correct faulty vision or not, have become a fashion statement of their own. Such was not always the case. At one time, wearing eyeglasses was thought to be a violation of God's law. A few centuries ago, an English clergyman wrote that "the newly invented optick glasses are immoral, since they prevent the natural light, and make things appear in an unnatural and false light." The man who introduced **spectacles**, as eyeglasses were once called, to Italy, had this inscription carved on his tombstone.

Here lies Salvino d'Armato of Florence
Inventor of spectacles.
God pardon him his sins AD 1317

Life is indeed nicer in our own times.

Focus on Reading

1. If you were asked to design a pair of eyeglasses, what would they look like? Make a few sketches of your ideas.
2. Some people, especially children, feel embarrassed to wear eyeglasses. What would you say to a child to help convince him, or her, that eyeglasses were necessary?

3. Do you wear eyeglasses or contact lenses? If so, explain your choice.

7

Today, women have taken their rightful places at the highest levels of all walks of life. Yet, it remains unlikely that any woman will ever outdo the remarkable feats that Ida Lewis of Newport, Rhode Island, accomplished more than 100 years ago.

IDA LEWIS, AMERICAN HERO

Sixteen-year-old Ida Lewis knew something was wrong the moment she saw her mother standing in the doorway of their home. The trim white cottage stood on Lime Rock, a small island at the southern end of Newport Harbor. Attached to the house was a wooden tower topped by a lantern, the lighthouse. The lantern was a bright light and burned constantly, warning ships of the rocky shore nearby.

Just a few months earlier, in June 1857, Captain Hoseah Lewis had been named keeper of the Lime Rock Light. Soon after, he moved his family into the keeper's house and settled into the routine of life on a tiny island.

Now the Lewises were happy. For 12 years before the move, Hoseah Lewis had been a ship's captain. That meant long months away from his family every year. As lighthouse keeper, the family would be together again.

But on this October day, Idawalley Lewis's usual smiling face was not to be seen. Instead, she wore a troubled, saddened look. Young Ida could not hide her concern.

"Something is wrong, Mother," she cried. "What is it?"

"Your father has a serious illness, Ida."

"Is he . . . is he . . .?" Ida could not complete her thought.

"Hoseah will live, Ida, but he will never be strong enough to work again," her mother said.

Ida was relieved, but still worried. "What about the light? It must be kept burning!"

Ida's mother smiled through her sorrow. She expected such concern from her daughter. From the earliest, Ida always felt the responsibility of keeping the light burning. "And it will, Ida, it will! I shall do what I can, of course, but with taking care of Hoseah and the rest of our family, I may not be able to do it all. I shall count on you, Ida, since you are the oldest."

So, young Ida Lewis took over the duties of tending to the light. It would be nearly 50 years before she stopped. Why then? "Because I am getting old, I guess," Ida said, "and I really can't handle a boat like I used to."

Handle a boat? As Ida's father had once told a reporter: "She knew how to handle a boat, hold onto the wind, and fight a gale better than any man I ever saw wet an oar, and do it, too, when the sea was breaking over her."

At first, Ida merely did the work of her father, but when he died in 1872, Congress passed a special act naming Ida keeper of the light on Lime Rock. By the time she passed on the job to her brother Rudolph, when she was 64 years old, Ida was officially credited with saving 23 people with her little skiff. Twenty-three people and one sheep, that is. What is more, she won fame the world over, was awarded a number of medals for her rescues, and became the highest paid lighthouse keeper on the East Coast.

In those days, lighthouses were not powered by electricity as they are today. Lime Rock's light was lighted by an oil-soaked wick. Twice a day young Ida had to climb the tower to trim the wick so the light would burn steadily. She also polished the glass mirrors that reflected the light into the harbor. She also pumped the oil from a ground-level tank high up to the fountain that held the wick.

Nor were those her only duties. Every day, no matter what the weather was like, Ida rowed her younger brothers and sister to school on the mainland. She shopped for food and for supplies for the light, all of which she carried back to Lime Rock in her skiff. Then there were chores like helping to cook, clean up, and keep the house neat—inside and out.

All that may sound like hard and tiresome work, but not to Ida. Even as a small child, she decided that playing games like tag or whizz, or rolling hoops like other children her age were not for her. Ida much preferred rowing a small boat around the harbor, helping fishermen haul their catches, or swimming miles on end. By the time she was 12, she could outrow anyone in Newport. At 14, she was the best swimmer as well, nor was she shy about telling anyone how good she was—something her father did not like.

"Boasting is not becoming in a young lady," he often reminded her.

Her usual answer went something like this. "But I was the best, Father, and I still am. I am as good at things of the sea as any man, and I do not care who knows it!"

Ida made her first rescue when she was still 16. Four young boys were sailing a small boat out of the harbor when one of them suddenly climbed the mast. The extra weight high up flipped the boat over. All four boys were tossed into the cold water.

Lucky for them Ida was watching from the lighthouse. When the boat went over, she dashed to her skiff, slid it into the water, and rowed furiously to the youngsters, now thoroughly scared as well as wet and cold.

Ida carefully maneuvered the stern, or back end, of her skiff near each boy in turn, hauling them, one by one, over the stern and into the boat. Rowing them back to shore, Ida recognized one of the boys. It was John King, the one who had climbed the mast. She let him know what she thought of that.

"That was quite a foolish thing you did, John. You know you could have drowned—all of you!"

"It was, Ida," John answered. "And it was all my fault. I was just showing off."

"Well, John King, the next time you have an urge to show off in front of your friends, do it on shore."

"I will, Ida, I promise," John said. He waited a moment, then pleaded, "Ida, you won't tell our parents about this, will you? They'd never let us go sailing again!"

Ida studied their worried faces before she answered. "All right, boys, this time I won't tell. But believe me, if there ever is a next time . . . "

True to her word, Ida never told the boys' parents. Nor was that the only time she kept her rescues a secret. A few years later, Ida watched a boat carrying three soldiers from nearby Fort Adams turn over and sink. Two of the men began swimming for shore while the third clung desperately to a piece of driftwood.

Ida rowed as fast as she could and reached the soldier before he slipped under the water. But he was too big for her to haul into the skiff. So she tied a line around him and, rowing slowly, towed him to safety. Near shore she called to a fisherman, who helped get the soldier onto the beach.

Once the soldier was rested enough to talk, Ida asked him about the boat his friends were using. In the soldier's own words, "they had borrowed it." What is worse, the boat belonged to Ida's brother.

"It doesn't matter now," Ida said. "The boat is at the bottom of the harbor. You shall have to answer to Rudolph later."

Ida then realized the soldier was still exhausted from the near drowning. "Right now you need some rest and warm, dry clothes. You look to be about the same size as Rudolph. Rest here while I get you some of his things."

Dressed in her brother's clothes, the grateful soldier returned to Fort Adams. Ida never told his commanding officer what the soldier had done. Quite likely, the soldier never paid for the lost skiff, either, as he never did return the borrowed clothes. As for his two friends who chose to swim for shore, their fate remains a mystery.

Over the next several years Ida saved many more lives. Not all of these rescues were unnoticed or unrewarded. Often friends of those she saved took up a collection of money to reward her. One year the town of Newport presented Ida with a new skiff, the finest that could be built.

By 1869, when Ida was 27 years old, she had been credited with saving 11 lives. She was given silver medals and had her picture and story in the country's leading magazines. Now she was a national celebrity.

That same year, President Ulysses S. Grant, along with Vice-President Schuyler Colfax, visited Ida on Lime Rock. As they landed on the island, President Grant stepped out of the boat into water up to his knees.

"I have come to see Ida Lewis," he said, "and to see her I'd get wet up to my armpits if necessary."

The President and Ida had a long chat, during which he asked her which rescue stood out in her mind. The normally shy Ida laughed and said, "That has to be the time I saved a sheep."

The president looked very surprised. "You mean you risked your life to save a . . . sheep?"

Ida giggled. "It was worth it, too. You see, these three men were driving a prize sheep through town when the animal suddenly bolted. It ran off the Old Mill Wharf and fell into the water. The men took after it in a boat, quite ignoring the heavy storm that was blowing at the time.

"They had just about reached the poor creature when a huge wave swamped their boat, filling it up with water. I rowed out and fished them out of the water. Yet, they were more upset about the lost of the sheep than about themselves. So I went after it. That took about an hour of heavy rowing against the storm, but I saved their sheep."

"And the men you saved?" President Grant asked.

"Oh, they were grateful," Ida said. "They told me I had saved their jobs as well as their lives!"

When the President stopped chuckling, Vice-President Schuyler Colfax spoke up. "Miss Lewis," he said, "I can't for the life of me understand how anyone would want to spend a lifetime on a tiny rock pile on the ocean. Aren't you ever lonely?"

"Alone occasionally, Mr. Colfax, but never lonely. I am quite happy. You see, there is a peace on these rocks that you don't get on shore. What is more, there are hundreds of boats going in and out of this harbor each summer. It is part of my happiness to know they are depending on me to guide them safely."

After the President's visit, Ida went on tending the light and rescuing people for 37 more years. At the age of 64, she turned the duties over to her brother Rudolph. Still, people in great numbers came out to Lime Rock to visit her. As many as came in a single day to get a look at Ida. They came not only from nearby towns cities, but from places all over the country, and indeed, all over the world.

Despite her apparent strong health, Ida suffered from heart disease for many years. On October 12, 1911, she—like her father earlier—suffered a stroke. On the day she was taken sick, the commanding officer of Fort Adams suspended all cannon firing practice. "Our Ida needs peace and quiet," he explained. Less than two weeks later, on October 24, Ida Lewis died. She was 69 years old.

Praise from all over the world flowed into Newport. They came from presidents and kings, from queens and leaders of industry, as well as from ordinary folk. Yet, none was so elegantly simple or moving as that given by her Newport friends. Having heard the news of her death, captains of ships anchored in the harbor began tolling their bells. The captains and their crews realized they had lost a true friend and a genuine American hero.

Focus on Reading

1. What traits of Ida Lewis do you admire? Would you have liked to have known her? Explain why, or why not.
2. In your mind, what makes a hero? Does Ida Lewis qualify?
3. The selection shows that Ida was a responsible person, even from a very young age. Point out some examples to support this.

8

Every day countless numbers of people drink Coca-Cola, travel on Greyhound buses, use safety razors, nibble on pretzels. Did you ever wonder how these four very popular things came to be?

Stories Behind the Names

Coca-Cola

Is there any soft drink more widely known or liked around the world than Coca-Cola? Quite likely, no. Indeed, more than one person has pointed out that Coca-Cola rivals the flag itself as a symbol of America to the rest of the world.

The story of Coca-Cola, or Coke as it has been called for more than 70 years, begins in Atlanta, Georgia, in 1866. That was the year a man named John S. Pemberton opened a drugstore. As a businessman, Pemberton was something of a failure. One reason was that he spent more time trying to mix up new medicines than he did tending to his customers. When none of these ideas worked out, Pemberton shifted to trying to create a new soft drink.

He fiddled with any number of formulas using a variety of ingredients, searching for a new taste. Nothing worked—until May 1886. That was the year Pemberton finally got the taste he wanted.

The next step was to mix up a larger batch. He did this in an old iron pot over a wood fire in the backyard of his Atlanta home. Pemberton cooled the batch, tasted it, and smiled. Here was a taste he liked! But what should he name his new drink?

The naming was left up to his friend and business partner, Frank M. Robinson. Robinson put together the names of two of the many ingredients in the mix. One ingredient was *coca*, dried leaves of a South American bush. The other was *cola*, a flavor extracted, or squeezed, out of the Kola nut. The result: Coca-Cola.

Now that Pemberton had a name for his soft drink, he set out to sell the product. He talked owners of some drugstores in Atlanta into taking some Coca-Cola syrup on trial. They did, and people took an instant liking to the syrup mixed with carbonated water. That first year Pemberton sold 25 gallons of syrup. The new company was on its way to greatness, but not with John S. Pemberton.

Pemberton died in 1888, just two years after Coca-Cola came on the market. Another druggist, Asa G. Candler, bought the entire company for just $2,300! Candler helped the business grow so that in seven short years he could claim that "Coca-Cola is now sold in every state in the country."

The next big step in the growth of the company came from the outside. Until 1900, Candler sold only the syrup. Then a lawyer from Tennessee, named Benjamin F. Thomas, got the idea to sell Coca-Cola in bottles. Thomas and a friend talked Asa Candler into trying their idea. They opened the first bottling plant in Tennessee (at a cost of $5,000). It was an immediate success. Soon bottling plants opened up all over the country. Each of these was—and is—individually owned and run.

The owners buy the syrup from the main company and mix it and bottle it themselves. What ingredients go into the syrup, only a handful of people know. Their secret is guarded as closely as any government's secrets.

How loyal are Coke drinkers? A lot more loyal than even the top officers of the company once thought. A few years ago, Coca-Cola tinkered with the original formula and brought out something called "New Coke." The public was outraged that anyone would change their favorite soft drink. Shocked officials at the Atlanta headquarters of Coca-Cola were buried by protests. They gave in and started making the original flavor again. Coke drinkers were happy, and the people who ran the company learned an important lesson: Don't try to change a winner!

Greyhound

The American dream has always meant anyone can better his or her life. To many people, this means starting a business of their own. That was what young Carl Eric Wickman did nearly 80 years ago.

Wickman was a miner in the iron-mining region of Minnesota. The work was hard and dangerous, though, and it paid very little. In short, young Wickman knew mining didn't hold much of a future for him. So he quit his job in order to start selling automobiles in 1914.

Unfortunately, the car he chose to sell was called the Hupmobile. To say the least, this was not one of the more popular cars of its time. Wickman did not sell a single Hupmobile his first year in business. His dream of a better life was disappearing fast, but he was determined not to go back to mining.

What Wickman did was use the seven-passenger Hupmobile he owned as a jitney, or small bus. For 15 cents (a quarter round trip), he drove miners the 4 miles between the Minnesota towns of Hibbing and Alice. The very first day he took in $2.25—more than he earned sweating in the mines.

Wickman's jitney bus caught on quickly, and soon he had trouble carrying all the minors who preferred to ride to work, rough and dangerous though the trip was. He added two more seats to his Hupmobile and even had eager riders hanging on to the sides of the bus!

Now Wickman talked a friend into joining his business. Together they bought a second Hupmobile, fitted it with ten seats, and added new routes. Within a year, the two men started the very first long-distance bus route. This was the 90 miles between Hibbing and Duluth.

If the short trip between Hibbing and Alice was dangerous, the new, longer route was even more risky. There were no superhighways in 1915—indeed, there were few paved roads anywhere. Besides, Minnesota's long, cold winters didn't make travel any easier. In fact, the Hupmobile on this route carried snow shovels and strong ropes so passengers could free the bus from the usual icy slides going into snowbanks. Passenger comforts included woolen blankets and hot bricks on the floor to keep their feet warm!

All these jitneys were painted grey, which did not show dust and dirt as easily as other colors. They also had a long, lean look they got from adding a few feet onto the car bodies. These facts led to a name for the new business.

A hotel owner who watched the Hupmobiles pass his place every day told Carl Wickman they reminded him of "greyhound dogs streaking by."

Wickman was pleased with that picture, so he named his company the Greyhound Bus Lines. He also thought up an advertisement: "Ride the Greyhounds."

From that simple beginning, Greyhound grew into the world's biggest inter-city passenger carrier. Today thousands of its buses move people more than half a *billion* miles each year. Carl Wickman's dream was fulfilled.

Gillette Safety Razor

The person who, it has been said, "changed the face of men" was King C. Gillette, the inventor of the safety razor.

Until the Gillette razor came on the scene in 1901, shaving one's face was, at best, a painful experience. At worst, it could be dangerous. The accepted way was to shave with a straight razor, variations of which go back thousands of years to the ancient Egyptians. The straight razor was a very sharp single blade like a knife about 4 inches long. (Another way to get rid of beards was to do what some Native American tribes in the Northeast did. They simply removed their beards by pinching the hairs between clam shells and pulling them out.)

The straight razor took a fair amount of practice to use properly. One error could result in a healthy slice of skin taken off the face. This is one reason why so many men in Gillette's time grew beards. Of course, people could always go to a barber for a daily shave in those days. But barbers cost money, and not everyone could afford the luxury. Then, along came Gillette.

Although Gillette had been a traveling salesman from the time he was 17 years old, selling was not his real interest. Inventing things was. He was rather good at thinking up ideas for new and better things, too, but he never had enough money to get his inventions to the marketplace. Then one day, Gillette's boss said to him: "King, you're always inventing something. Why don't you concentrate on one thing, something that people use once and then throw away?"

Gillette thought that was good advice. He focused on the idea—"something that people use once and then throw away." How to develop that idea into a useful product did not come easily for Gillette. When it did, though, it came in a flash.

"One morning when I started to shave, I found my straight razor needed sharpening. That meant it would have to be taken to a barber. 'A razor is only a sharp edge,' I said to myself, 'and all that's back of it is just support. Why do they go to all the expense and trouble of fashioning a backing that has nothing to do with shaving? They could get the same result by putting an edge on a piece of steel only thick enough to hold an edge.'" Gillette stood there before his mirror, letting the idea take shape in his mind—and it did, quickly.

"In that moment, I saw it all. The way the blade could be held in a holder. The idea of sharpening the two opposite edges on the thin piece of steel. The holders for the blade. The handle halfway between the two edges of the blade."

Gillette called his invention the safety razor and took it around to people he thought would want to invest in the idea. He was wrong. Rather than give Gillette money to start a business, they laughed at him.

Gillette struggled on for years, tinkering with his safety razor, begging people for money at the same time. Along the way he learned he would need a special kind of steel, much more costly than he thought. And all the while people were urging him to give up his foolish idea. "I didn't know enough to quit," Gillette later explained. "I was a dreamer in search of the gold at the foot of the rainbow."

In 1901 Gillette finally found money. Friends gave him $5,000 to start his company. Two years later (after spending another $7,000 he had to borrow), the first razors were introduced. Gillette sold 51 safety razors and 168 blades in the first year. A slow start, yes, but the next year, 1901, he sold more than 100,000 razors and many more blades than that! The Gillette Safety Razor had been accepted by the public. Shaving would never be the same again.

Pretzels

If you're like most people, you like pretzels. Some people prefer the large, soft pretzels, served hot, dripping in mustard. Others like the small, crisp pretzels right out of a box. Either way, pretzels are a favorite snack food. Each year Americans consume hundreds of millions of pounds of the tasty treat.

Look closely at a pretzel the next time you're about to take a bite of one. It has a distinctive shape. There is a story behind that shape. What is more, the lowly pretzel has an uncommon history. It once helped save an entire city from destruction!

The pretzel was created by an unknown Italian priest many hundreds of years ago. This unknown priest wanted to reward little children for learning their prayers. So he devised the pretzel in the shape of a child's arms folded in prayer. (The name *pretzel* itself likely comes from an old Latin word, *pretiola*, meaning "small gift.")

By the 1500s, people all over the continent of Europe were enjoying pretzels. It was then that the pretzel earned its place in history.

Early in the 1500s, bands of fierce Turkish warriors roamed Europe. It was feared they would soon conquer the entire continent. Finally, though, they were stopped at the walled city of Vienna.

Try as they could, the Turks could not break through the walls. Then they devised a plan. They would tunnel under the walls at night and gain entrance to Vienna that way. Their plan would have worked—except for the pretzel bakers of the city.

You see, they worked at night, too, cooking pretzels for the next day's sale. Hearing the digging, the bakers alerted the army, who once more beat back the Turks. That was enough for the Turks. They left Europe. As a reward, the pretzel bakers were awarded their own coat of arms. A coat of arms is a design with animals and objects, such as lions or horses, flowers or swords, that represents an important person, an organization (such as a union or a business) or of an institution (such as a school, a college, or a church). For the pretzel bakers to have their own coat of arms was a great honor. What did it contain? Its design featured pretzels, of course.

Focus on Reading

1. Each of the episodes in the article tells a success story. What good character traits did you find each person had? How did these character traits help the person succeed?
2. Do you think any of the persons in the stories would be successful today? Explain why, or why not.
3. What new product do you think the world needs today? Think of a name for your product and tell why the world needs it.

9

A lot of folklore has its roots in real people and real events. As the stories are told and retold over the years they change in many ways, making them perhaps less believable (though perhaps funnier). So it is with the story of Thomas Smith, dreamer of great dreams.

THOMAS SMITH AND HIS WINDWAGON

Nowadays, should you want to travel from Missouri to California, you can board a jet plane and be there in a matter of hours. Of course, that was not always true. Take the year 1853, for example. There were no airplanes then. There was no railroad to California. There were not even any automobiles. The only way was to make the trip on horseback or as part of a wagon train. With luck, you would get there in a few months.

You might guess, then, that people were looking for a way to shorten that boring, often dangerous journey, and you would be right. That is why, one pleasant spring day, Thomas Smith and his wife, Sarah, stopped their strange-looking wagon on the main street of Westport, Missouri. In moments a crowd of curious townspeople gathered round.

"What in tarnation you riding there, mister?" a man called out. "That's the oddest looking wagon I ever did see."

Thomas looked out at the sea of faces. A childlike glint showed in his eyes as he began to speak. Thomas's wife saw the glint, too. She rolled her eyes and gave her husband a here-we-go-again look. Thomas missed it completely.

"Folks," he said, standing up in the wagon, "I see you have a look on your faces that says 'I don't believe what I saw.' Well, I want to assure you that what you saw *did* happen, just as sure as this is the year 1853. I, Thomas Smith, and my wife, Sarah, sailed this wagon to Westport. That's right, I said *sailed*!"

Thomas put a lot of emphasis on the word *sailed*. In fact, stressing words he felt were important was a habit with him. He was about to go on when another man called out from the assembled crowd.

"Where's the oxen, Smith?" the man demanded. "I ain't never seen a wagon that big without a team of oxen to pull it. And what's that blanket, the one flapping on the pole?"

"There are no oxen, my friend," Thomas laughed. "That's the point. And that blanket is a *sail*. And the pole it's hanging from is a *mast*." Thomas then pointed to another, shorter pole, this one attached to the back of the wagon. "And this here's a tiller. It's what we use to steer boats with back in New England, where we come from."

"You've been out in the sun too long, mister. You're plain crazy!" another voice cried out.

By now the crowd, which was still growing, was near doubled over in laughter. That made Thomas a bit angry. His face turned red, which only made everyone laugh louder. Now Thomas was really angry. He looked as if he was about to take on the whole town in one grand fist fight. Sarah's only reaction was to pick up a book and begin reading. Just as she did a tall man stepped forward.

He wore a long black coat and striped trousers tucked into boots, a string tie, and a clean shirt. A wide-brimmed Stetson [cowboy] hat shaded his lined face from the prairie sun. The man brushed at his thick mustache with one hand and waved at the crowd with the other. Something in the way he held himself made them quiet down.

The man looked up at Thomas, who was clenching and unclenching his fists, trying to stay calm. Sarah sighed and turned the page in her book. The man spoke.

"I'm Doc Adams, head of the Town Council here in Westport," he said in a deep voice. "I'd like to hear what you have to say. Go ahead, young man, make your point."

Thomas looked relieved. "Thank you, sir," he began. "What I was about to say was I've been a sailor all my life. Well, I got to thinking the prairie's nothing more than a big, grassy ocean. There's hills like waves. There's canyons and gullies like harbors. Most of all there's the wind. It blows all the time."

"Ain't nothing you can tell us about the prairie wind, Smith," a man said. He was about to say more when Doc Adams stopped him dead with a withering look. Thomas went on.

"Well, then, why not let the wind push a wagon, I thought. It'd be cheaper than using oxen. And faster, too. Why, with your help, I can build a windwagon that will take you across the prairie so fast that you'll almost *be* where you want to go *before* you start!"

That drew a low murmur from the crowd and a response from Doc Adams. "That's some idea, young man," he said. "But actions speak louder than words around Westport. You've got to prove to us your idea will work before we agree to help."

Thomas smiled. "More than happy to oblige, sir. I'm off to Council Groves. Sarah will stay here in town with you good folks."

Sarah looked up from her book. She snatched up her luggage and stormed off the wagon. The look on her face was unmistakable. "I don't need you to tell me what I will or won't do, Thomas Smith," it said. Once again, Thomas paid no attention to her. He hauled up the sail. Tiller in one hand and a line controlling the sail in his other, Thomas got the windwagon moving. In minutes he was out of sight, carried along by the fresh prairie wind.

Doc Adams took off his hat and scratched his head. "Well, look at that, will you?" he said. "He sure seems to know what he's doing."

Sarah glared at Doc Adams; a tone of anger in her voice, she said: "And why not, Doctor? Thomas is no fool. He may be a dreamer, but at least he acts on his dreams."

Doc Adams looked surprised. "No harm meant, Mrs. Smith," he said. "It's just that, well, you've got to agree your husband and this windwagon invention are something quite, ah, different from what us folks in Westport are accustomed to seeing. I apologize if I offended you."

"Apology accepted, Doctor," Sarah answered. "But you just remember that it's dreamers like Thomas who will make this country grow. Like the poet said, 'We are the dreamers of dreams. We are the movers and shakers of the world.'"

Doc Adams looked like a little boy who'd been lectured to by a stern aunt. "Yes, ma'am, I'll keep that in mind," he said meekly.

Five days later, Thomas Smith sailed back into Westport. Sarah and Doc Adams were the first to greet him. Doc sounded shocked.

"You mean you drove or sailed clear over to Council Groves and back in just five days? Why, that's 150 miles. Each way!"

Thomas smiled a grand smile. "Would have made it sooner if I had a *better* wagon. This one just *fights* the wind." He held out an envelope. "This here's a letter from the mayor of Council Grove. It'll prove what I'm saying."

Doc Adams waved the letter aside. "No need to see that, Mr. Smith," he said. "I believe you."

Sarah shot Doc Adams one of her I-told-you-so looks. "See what I mean, Doctor?" she trumpeted. "My Thomas not only dreams. He *does*!"

"Doc Adams sighed. "I'm sure convinced, ma'am."

Within a few days, Thomas Smith and Doc Adams formed the Great Prairie Navigation Company. Their idea was to build a whole fleet of windwagons, which they'd sell to travelers heading to California.

"We'll be rich as kings, Doc, rich as *kings*!" Thomas sang out. "*Everyone* will want one of our windwagons!"

Work began at once, with nearly the whole town pitching in to help. Soon the first windwagon began to take shape.

"This one's going to be a whole lot bigger than mine," Thomas boasted, holding the plans out to an onlooker.

"Looks to be about 40 feet long," the man said.

"Right. And *10* feet wide. And the wheels will be *12* feet apart," Thomas added proudly.

"With axles big as *tree trunks*!" Doc Adams added, emphasizing words as he spoke, just the way Thomas Smith did.

Though it was in fact a wagon, Thomas Smith's latest wagon looked a lot like a small ship. It had a deck to walk on and a mast 30 feet tall to hold the sail. It even had a figurehead up front, just the way any proper sailing vessel would. Sarah was impressed enough to comment about it.

"Thomas," she said brightly, "your carved figurehead of a Sioux warrior looks wonderful!"

Thomas smiled down at his wife from his perch on the deck of the windwagon. "You're right, Sarah," he said. "And see how he's pointing the way. That was your idea, and a fine one it was."

"Well, *mine* was painting the wagon red, white, and blue," Doc Adams broke in.

"*Fine* colors," Thomas agreed.

Launching day was the biggest event Westport had ever held. People came from miles around to enjoy the party. A band played and cheers filled the air when a team of 20 oxen pulled the wagon to the edge of town. Thomas Smith stood proudly at the tiller, the huge sail flapping in the wind. A few of Westport's more important, and daring, citizens were on the wagon with him. Sarah had chosen to remain with her new-found friends rather than take a maiden voyage. Doc Adams passed up a chance to ride on *The Spirit of Westport*, as the windwagon was named, as well.

"I'll just follow along on my mule," he explained, holding up his medicine bag, "in the odd chance something goes wrong."

"*Perfect* day for a sail!" Thomas cried out. "*Free* up the oxen!"

Two men unhitched the oxen and led them aside. Wind filled the huge sail, and Thomas's windwagon sailed off, lurching up hills and swaying through gullies. Doc Adams could hardly keep them in sight.

What the ride lacked in smoothness, it more than made up for in speed. The passengers, not used to anything faster than an oxen-drawn wagon, held on for dear life. Thomas Smith never looked happier.

"Watch this, folks," he laughed. "I'm going to turn us *through* the wind. Then we'll really *move*!"

Unfortunately, the heavy wagon never quite passed through the wind. Instead, it stopped turning with the wind directly in front of it and began to move backward. The passengers quickly sounded the alarm. "The other way!" "Turn this thing around!" "Slow down! Slow down!" came the frightened cries.

In truth, Thomas tried his best to control the wagon, but the wind was too strong and the wagon too clumsy. The tiller snapped off in his hand, and the wagon began to sail round and round in circles. That seemed to slow things a bit, and, one by one, the terrified passengers leaped off.

"*Cowards*!" Thomas cried after them, all the while holding to the mast with a deathlike grip.

Thanks to a fence at the end of Gopher Creek, *The Spirit of Westport* finally crashed to a stop, upright. Doc Adams and the survivors quickly ran up. Thomas could see they were not in the best of moods.

"I'll have this fixed in no time, folks," he said, trying to sound cheerful. "We'll be ready to go again in a day or two at the *most.*"

Doc Adams spoke for everyone, and in a voice that, while calm, was still commanding. "I think we've had enough of this windwagon nonsense."

"But wait a minute, *please,*" Thomas begged. He wanted to go on pleading his case. The look on Doc Adams's face, though, told him in no uncertain terms the Great Prairie Navigation Company was no more.

For a moment Thomas Smith looked as if he'd cry. Then, just as suddenly, his face brightened. "Oh, well," he said, "Sarah and I was thinking about heading back *East* anyway. You see, I have this *other* idea. I'm going to put long skate blades on sailboats. Then people can *use* the frozen lakes and rivers in the winter. As a matter of fact, I'm thinking of calling my idea *iceboating.* What do you think of *that*, Doc?"

Doc Adams could only shake his head from side to side. Then he turned and walked slowly back to his waiting mule. The others followed along, leaving Thomas Smith alone, busily making sketches in the dirt by Gopher Creek.

Focus on Reading

1. Robert Browning, an English poet who lived more than 100 years ago, wrote that "a man's reach should exceed his grasp." How might that apply to Thomas Smith and his windwagon dream?

2. Virtually everyone has dreams. What are yours?
3. Although Sarah Smith, Thomas's wife, is not the main character in the story, we learn quite a bit about the kind of person she is. How would you describe her? How does she feel about her husband? How does he feel about her? Refer to specific parts of the story to support your opinions.

10

Prejudice comes in many forms. However, only one kind cuts across all lines to make one of the world's largest oppressed minorities: left-handed people.

It's Okay to Be a Lefty

Being a lefty isn't easy. Any left-handed person will tell you that this is a right-handed world. Objects from can openers to cameras are designed for right-handed people. Want to learn to play the guitar? Unless you are fortunate enough to find one of the few models for lefties (and can afford one), you have few options. You can (a) play it upside-down, with the bass strings on top; (b) restring the instrument (not an easy thing to do successfully); or (c) learn to play like a right-handed musician.

Even a simple task like writing favors right-handed people. They write smoothly, pulling the pen or pencil along the paper. A left-handed person has to push the pen or pencil. (Forget about using most fountain pens—pens that use ink. The nibs, or pen points, on these are almost always designed for right-handed people.) One result of pushing the writing instrument is that lefties tend to write more slowly. A second is that the lefty's moving hand is likely to slide over the writing, smudging what he or she has already written.

Even ordinary language works against left-handed people. The word *left* itself comes from an Old English word meaning "weak" or "worthless." The German word for *left* means "awkward" or "clumsy." The French meaning of the word for *left (gauche)* is also "awkward" or "crooked," and if you are *zurdo* [SUR doh] in Spain—that is left-handed—you are also "clumsy."

What did left-handed people do to deserve all this prejudice? Quite likely, nothing. Yet prejudice against lefties is about as old as recorded history itself. For example, ancient Romans centuries ago believed that the right foot should always come before the left. Putting on the left sandal first or entering the house with the left foot forward was sure to bring bad luck, they thought. Over the years some people even associated the left side of the body with the Devil and evil spirits.

A number of folk superstitions support the idea that the right side is the lucky side. For example, a buzzing in your right ear means someone is praising you. On the other hand, a buzzing in the left ear means someone is speaking badly of you. If your right foot itches, you will be going on a successful journey. But if you get out of bed on the wrong (left) side in the morning, you are in for a bad day.

As if all this were not bad enough, it now seems that left-handed people have even more to worry about. One recent scientific study revealed that left-handed people even die younger than right-handed people! According to this study, the life expectancy of left-handed women is about five years less than it is for right-handed women. For men, the results were even worse. Left-handed men have a life expectancy of *ten* years less (62 years to 72 years) than right-handed men. (That's even worse than the seven-year difference between smokers and nonsmokers.)

One reason for the difference in life expectancy may be that left-handed people are more likely to die in accidents. Could that be because we live in a world where almost everything is designed for right-handed people?

The news for left-handed people is not all bad, however. Some scientists believe that lefties are better at picturing ideas in their minds. This is a most useful trait in sciences such as physics and chemistry, and also in engineering ("What will happen to the flow of traffic on the bridge if I put the on-ramp here?" the design engineer asks himself.) It may also explain why so many left-handed people make superior artists, architects, and athletes.

Indeed, despite the prejudice that left-handed people are clumsy, the opposite is more often true. Many lefties have excelled at work that requires special skill and grace. Some of the world's greatest artists were left-handed: Michelangelo and Leonardo da Vinci, for example.

Playing a sport and being left-handed can actually be an advantage. Tennis players such as Martina Navratilova and John McEnroe put a deadly spin on the ball that right-handed players find hard to hit. Some of the best baseball players were lefties–Babe Ruth, Fernando Valenzuela, and Ricky Henderson, to name a few. (You may have noticed, though, that being a lefty in a game like golf is a decided disadvantage. Golf courses are always designed for right-handed players. As a result, nearly all professional golfers play right-handed. Even natural lefties are taught to play the other way.)

For years, scientists have been trying to learn why some people are left-handed while others are right-handed. Some scientists believe it is merely a matter of training, and, in fact, a child can be trained to use one hand or the other. But more and more studies show that people are born with a preference. (For example, some babies at birth prefer to suck their left thumb rather than their right. These same babies are more likely to turn their heads to the left than to the right. As you might guess, they are the "natural" lefties.)

There are more than 20 million lefties (or "southpaws," as they are sometimes called) in the United States alone—that is a big market! Finally, left-handed people are being noticed by manufacturers.

At long last, more appliances and tools are being designed especially for left-handed people. These include common items such as irons and ironing boards, playing cards, potato peelers, scissors—and even bank checkbooks. (Now, if car makers would only put some attention to making their products easier and safer for lefties!)

Why, lefties even have their own club—Left-handers International. It may be time for lefties to start feeling better about themselves and their world. The future looks good.

Focus on Reading

1. The selection mentions several common products that have begun to be designed for left-handed people. What other common objects might be adapted for left-handed people? Ask someone you know who is left-handed what things might be designed for lefties.
2. The main idea of a selection sums up what the story is about. In a single sentence tell the main idea of this selection.
3. Other than the examples given in the selection, when might being left-handed be an advantage? When would it be a decided disadvantage?

11

Women who are qualified should not be kept from holding any office people believed. But did that include leading an important Native American nation?

Cherokee Leader

Mankiller is not an ordinary surname. But then Wilma P. Mankiller is not an ordinary woman. She got her unusual last name from an ancestor—a Cherokee warrior who lived more than 100 years ago. For a good part of her own life, Wilma Mankiller has been a warrior of sorts, fighting for a better life for her people.

Wilma's people are the 108,000 Cherokees who make up the second largest Native American nation in the United States. Since 1985, she has been the principal chief of this nation—the first woman to serve in that position in any major Native American group.

Here is an enormous job. She compares it to "running a small country." Headquartered in Tahlequah, Oklahoma, the Cherokee nation has an annual budget of $52 million. It runs businesses, social welfare programs, and health clinics. It employs 1,700 tribal workers. Yet, the popular but wrong ideas about Native Americans continue to exist.

"There are so many forces working against our people," Wilma explains. "There are people . . . who don't realize our communities exist as they do today. Most people like to deal with us though we were in a museum or a history book."

If anyone is likely to change that view of Native Americans, it is Wilma Mankiller.

One of 11 children, Wilma grew up on a farm in eastern Oklahoma. The land she and her family lived on had been given to her grandfather by the government. However, like most Native Americans, the Mankillers were poor. Their house had no electricity, no heat, no bathrooms.Yet, Wilma says, "We didn't think we were particularly bad off because everyone we knew was in the same situation."

Her father knew better, however. After two years of drought that killed the crops, it was hard just to put food on the table, let alone make a living off the farm.

When Wilma was 11 years old, her father decided to take advantage of a new program offered by the Bureau of Indian Affairs (BIA) in Washington, D.C. The program would move Native American families into cities. The idea was to get Native Americans to places where there were jobs so that they could have a better standard of living. According to Wilma, "The BIA . . thought that if they could take all the Native Americans from their tribal community and move them to a city, it would solve all their social problems." It did not.

San Francisco seemed like another planet. To children who had never even seen a television, the city was full of problems and dangers. What is more, "Both my mother and father felt like outcasts," Wilma said later. Still, the program did teach the Native Americans one lesson which was this: leaving their own lands did not solve their problems.

Despite all this, Wilma did struggle on and finished high school. Then she became a social worker, married, and had two children. In 1969, Wilma came to a turning point in her life.

To bring attention to the plight of their people, a group of young Native Americans took over Alcatraz prison, once the most feared prison in America. During the occupation of the prison, which lasted 18 months, Wilma helped raise money to support the protestors.

"Those college students articulated a lot of feelings I had that I'd never been able to express," she said.

Being a mother prevented Wilma from joining the protestors, but, from then on, she became an activist for Native American rights. Wilma began taking college courses at night. During the day she worked on programs for Native Americans in the California school system.

No longer happy with her own life, Wilma divorced her husband, a businessman from South America. She moved back to her grandfather's land in Oklahoma with her two children. She built a small house on the property, called Mankiller Flats, and took her first job working in the Cherokee nation government. At the same time she continued taking college courses.

In 1979 she earned a college degree in social science. But that was not enough. "I felt bored with just putting together social programs," Wilma remembers, "and I wanted to figure out how to put together an entire community." With that in mind, she went back to college, this time to work toward a graduate degree—study beyond college.

A second turning point in Wilma's life occurred shortly after this. Driving home from classes one day she was badly injured in a head-on collision. Her car ran into another car coming straight at her. The driver of the other car, a friend, was killed. Wilma went through the agony of 17 operations to correct her injuries. As if that were not enough, she learned she had muscular dystrophy, a disease that destroys the muscles. Treatment for this disease involved painful doses of chemotherapy—a treatment of disease that uses drugs. Yet somehow, Wilma survived and emerged an even a stronger person.

"In a way it seems it was a test of perseverance or something that I went through," she says. "It was a kind of maturing process. It was a definite preparation."

Wilma Mankiller had fought her own personal battle and had won. Now she put her energy into another kind of battle—helping her people become self-sufficient. Wilma believes there is "tremendous potential for people to solve their own problems, given half a chance." She set out to see the Cherokees got that "half a chance."

At that time, two of the biggest problems in the Cherokee communities were a lack of water and bad housing. Wilma knew simply getting water to the villages and improving the houses were not enough. She had to convince the Cherokees they could help themselves toward a better life.

"The single most important thing in my work was trying to get people to maintain a sense of hope, and to see that they could come together and actually, physically, change their community."

Over the next few years, Wilma worked with her people for change. She helped raise funds for many projects. Water systems were improved and new homes were built. Health care and schools were upgraded. She showed the Cherokees how they could run their own businesses. Through her efforts, the once troubled town of Bell, Oklahoma, became a model community. Perhaps even more important, the Cherokees gained a new sense of pride.

"We used to be angry and upset—overwhelmed by social problems," one tribeswoman remembers. "But through Wilma's organizational skills and great personal commitment, we were able to realize better lives."

Wilma's success did not go unnoticed. Ross Swimmer, the main leader of the Cherokee nation, wanted her for his running mate for the tribe's election in 1983. Wilma thought long and hard about the offer.

"It meant making a transition from someone who is purely in a helping and enabling role to someone who has to go out and market herself. That is quite a transition."

Wilma also was not sure about running with Ross Swimmer. They had different ideas of how things should be done. But in the end, she decided to run. The most attractive reason for doing so, she said, was "getting into a position where I could make decisions about development and the things I believed in without having to ask somebody else about it."

It was a tough campaign. But that did not surprise Wilma as much as the reaction she met from the Cherokees. Many of her own people did not approve of her running! The reason had nothing to do with her views or her leadership skills. The problem was her sex.

Wilma was stunned and hurt. "I hadn't realized this would happen," she recalls. "I had built houses, I put in water systems, I knew heavy equipment. I had supervised carpenters and engineers, and I knew how a backhoe [a digging machine] operated. And no one ever said, 'You can't do that because you're a woman.' And yet when I wanted to move to a leadership position, all of a sudden people said, 'You can't do that because you're a woman.' It was quite a shock to me."

Wilma tried to focus on the issues in the campaign. It wasn't easy to do so. One day the tires on her car were slashed. She received a number of nasty telephone calls. Her life was even threatened. But on election day, the hard work she put in campaigning paid off. The Swimmer-Mankiller ticket was elected.

Wilma learned a lot during her first two years in office. She worked very hard. She knew she had to prove a woman could do the job. If one thing bothered her it was that she was still second in command. Then suddenly her break came. Ross Swimmer resigned to accept a job in Washington, D.C. with the BIA, and Wilma took his place. She became the first woman to lead the Cherokee nation.

Wilma's unique position drew a lot of attention. Just by being chief, she improved the image the outside world had of Native Americans. She was able to spread her message beyond the Cherokee nation. She showed people everywhere what could be accomplished through hard work and cooperation.

In the next three years Wilma continued to work for improvements in Cherokee communities. More than just a skilled businesswoman, she showed great skill in managing and motivating people. When re-election time came in 1987, her talents were widely recognized and appreciated. She won a strong victory.

Wilma's re-election was the first of many victories for her. That same year she was named Newsmaker of the Year. She was voted one of the Women of the Year by *Ms.* magazine. She has been honored by both Harvard and Yale Universities, but none of these honors changed Wilma's life. She still lives in a simple house with her second husband, a Cherokee. She still drives a used car to work. She enjoys being a grandmother. If fame brought Wilma Mankiller any changes, it was the increased opportunity to further her goals for her people.

In 1990, she had a serious operation and spent time in a hospital. Wilma did not let this stop her for long. She returned to work, full of plans. One plan was about money that her people got from the U.S. government. Wilma soon signed an agreement giving the Cherokees complete control over their own budget.

When the June election came in 1991, Wilma thought about stepping aside. After nearly 14 years in power, she wondered if it might be "a good time to do something else." In the end, she couldn't resist running one more time. On June 15, 1991, Wilma received an astounding 83 percent of the vote!

For Chief Mankiller, it was a wonderful vote of confidence. Clearly, she had achieved her goal of bringing a new sense of purpose to the Cherokee nation.

Focus on Reading

1. "Cherokee Leader" offers a brief picture of Wilma Mankiller. Having read the article, think of one word that best describes the kind of person she is. Refer to specific parts of the article to support your choice.
2. Choose another title for the article. Explain why you picked the title.
3. Wilma was shocked when people told her "You can't do that because you're a woman." Should she have been? Tell why, or why not.

Answers

1 How Wisdom Was Spread Throughout the World

1. Ananse shows a kind of intelligence that might make him seem wise when he takes great care in hiding his wisdom: he has a huge pot made, which is baked hard; it has a very small opening that he could seal shut and he ties the stopper tight with strong vines; he plans to hide the pot deep in the forest up in a tall tree with spikes on its trunk so that the tree is hard to climb. In fact, however, his efforts to hide the wisdom seem stupid and funny; his real wisdom is his recognition at the end of the story that "owning" wisdom in this way makes no sense and that he has less common sense than his little son. His greed is shown by the same effort to keep the wisdom of the world all for himself and let no one else have any of it.
2. Answers will vary. See answer to question 1.
3. The lesson Ananse learns is that "owning" a secret treasure of wisdom is not really wise; what is important is having good judgment in your life. You could apply this to everyday life by saying that it is more important to have practical knowledge and good judgment (such as the knowing the best way to carry a big pot) than it is to possess a body of knowledge that has no use except to make the person "owning" it feel superior.

2 Oak Island's Mysterious Money Pit

1. The main risks involved in digging for the treasure were the flooding of the deep hole the men dug and the risk of losing a lot of money paying for the work.
2. Answers will vary.
3. Answers will vary. The lesson might be that the pursuit of quick riches is a waste, since none of the people described ever found a single thing of value.

3 Get Garrett Morgan!

1. Garrett Morgan showed courage by going down into the burning tunnel with the men he had given gas masks. You also could say that he showed courage by continuing to sell his gas masks, and to invent other useful things, in spite of the racial prejudice he faced.
2. Garrett Morgan hired white men to demonstrate his gas masks so that the prejudiced people would not know that an African American was their inventor and manufacturer. In short, he reacted with determination and shrewdness. Since he clearly was not frightened by this hurtful rejection of him as a human being, and by this threat to his business, he also showed courage.
3. Answers will vary.

4 Stamps for Americans

1. Answers may vary.
2. Answers may vary.
3. Answers may vary.

5 Sawing Off Manhattan Island

1. Answers will vary.
2. Answers will vary.
3. Answers will vary.

6 How Eyeglasses Help You See

1. Answers will vary.
2. Answers will vary.
3. Answers will vary.

7 Ida Lewis, American Hero

1. Answers will vary. Admirable traits of Ida that might be mentioned are her outspokenness (if she was the best at something, she said so), her courage (in rescuing people—and sheep—in dangerous seas), her kindness (she did not report the boys who fell in the sea to their parents; she did not report the soldier who stole her brother's boat to his commanding officer). She also showed courage in doing a man's job when prejudice against women in male jobs was even stronger than it is today.
2. Answers will vary.
3. Ida showed responsiblity mainly by taking over her father's job as lighthouse keeper. Responsibility was also shown in all the rescues she made (see answer to question 1). The respect all the boat owners felt for her shows that she was considered an exceptionally responsible, reliable lighthouse keeper who could be counted on to protect their safety and help them when in need.

8 Stories Behind the Names

1. Pemberton, the inventor of Coca-Cola, and Gillette, the inventor of the safety razor, both showed great determination by continuing to believe in their new products when people laughed at their ideas and at first would not invest in them. Both of these inventors, as well as Wickman, the founder of the Greyhound Bus Line, showed curiosity and cleverness in trying out new ways of doing things—mixing different liquids until the right taste for a new soft drink was discovered, figuring out the design for a new razor that "people would use once and throw away," fixing up an unpopular car, the Hupmobile, so that it could seat more passengers and could be used as a bus.
2. Answers will vary.
3. Answers will vary.

9 Thomas Smith and His Windwagon

1. Thomas Smith illustrates the quotation because he was reaching for new ways to travel on land by using wind-and-sail power, which previously had been used only on lakes, rivers, and at sea. With the windwagon, he could not quite grasp his goal. At the end of the story, he was reaching for another kind of wind-and-sail power: the use of sailboats with ice skate blades on them, which would travel over frozen lakes and rivers. It was possible that with the new "iceboat" invention he might grasp the goal he was reaching for.
2. Answers will vary.
3. Sarah is loyal to her husband and supports his ideas. However, at times she turns her attention away from him when he gets into angry quarrels with people who doubt his ideas. When they first arrive in Westport, Missouri, and the people find the windwagon very strange, she "rolled her

eyes, and gave her husband a here-we-go-again look." When the windwagon surprises Doc Adams by actually sailing in the wind, she tells Doc Adams, "a tone of anger in her voice," that Thomas is a dreamer who acts on his dreams. She says essentially the same thing when Thomas success - fully returns from this first journey. On the other hand, when the people laugh at Thomas and he gets violently angry, "Sarah's only reaction was to pick up a book and begin reading." When he is "clenching and unclenching his fists, trying to stay calm," "Sarah sighed and turned the page in her book." She also gets very angry when he tells the crowd he will sail the wagon to another town while she will stay with them. She "stormed off the wagon. The look on her face was unmistakable. 'I don't need you to tell me what I will or won't do, Thomas Smith,' it said. Once again, he paid no attention to her." Thomas also does not notice her 'here-we-go-again' look mentioned above. However, he happily gives her credit for the idea of putting a figurehead on the windwagon. In conclusion: Sarah admires and loves her husband but gets frustrated with his behavior at times—his anger and his ignoring of her. Thomas regards Sarah as a partner—they are a team—and appreciates her support, but sometimes does not consider her feelings or ignores her.

10 It's Okay to Be a Lefty

1. Answers will vary. Objects designed for right-handers which are hard for left-handed people to use are: door handles; car door handles; gear-shift levers in cars; car ignitions; single-unit school desks; refrigerator doors; notebooks.
2. The main idea of the article might be stated as follows: Left-handed people still face widespread prejudice, despite their achievements and despite improved treatment of them by the right-handed world.

3. Answers will vary. In baseball, left-handers cannot be the shortstop, second baseman, or third baseman because they would have to turn halfway around to throw the ball to anyone in the infield. Catchers also are not supposed to be left-handed, though there have been some. Left-handed batters are even thought to have an advantage because pitchers have to adjust to them.

11 Cherokee Leader

1. Wilma Mankiller's three main traits seem to be her constant growth as a person as she saw new goals she wanted to reach, her ability to change her life so she could reach these goals, and her ability to overcome opposition in order to achieve a goal. Once she was inspired by the Native American college student protest, she started taking college courses, divorced her husband, moved back to her people's land, and began working for the Native American government. Then she went back to graduate school (study beyond college) so she could learn how to put together a bigger program for her people. To continue schooling, she had to overcome injuries from a terrible automobile accident. Then she had to overcome the passive attitude of her own people in order to teach them how to build up their community independently. Finally, she had to overcome the opposition of some of the Cherokees to having a woman be president of their government. In this last phase, she had to make a big change from being a helper and 'enabler' to being a political leader who would "go out and market herself."
2. Answers will vary.
3. Answers will vary.